P9-DBI-486

F R A N K
L L O Y D
W R I G H T
CHICAGOLAND
P O R T F O L I O

Text & Photographs by
Thomas A. Heinz

GIBBS·SMITH
P
PUBLISHER

720.92
HEI

DF 6C PG ~C CDS JK pb SD

First edition
97 96 95 94 8 7 6 5 4 3 2 1

Text and photographs copyright © 1994 by Thomas A. Heinz
All rights reserved. No part of this book may be reproduced by any means whatsoever, without written permission from the publisher, except for brief excerpts quoted for the purpose of review.

This is a Peregrine Smith Book, published by
Gibbs Smith, Publisher
P.O. Box 667
Layton, Utah 84041

Cover photograph: Ward Willits House, Elevation, © 1994 by Thomas A. Heinz
Design by J. Scott Knudsen, Park City, Utah
Printed by Regent Publishing Services, Hong Kong

Library of Congress Cataloging–in–Publication Data

Heinz, Thomas A.
    Frank Lloyd Wright. Chicagoland / Thomas A. Heinz.
        p.   cm.
    ISBN 0-87905-598-7 :
    1. Prairie school (Architecture)—Illinois—Chicago metropolitan area. 2. Wright, Frank Lloyd, 1867-1959—Themes, motives.
    I. Title.
NA735.C4H45 1994
720 '.92—dc20   93-29286
                                                   CIP

INTRODUCTION

NEARLY A THIRD OF ALL OF WRIGHT'S works, many of which are considered to be his masterpieces, are concentrated in the Chicago area. Most of these structures were built before 1910 and are fast approaching one hundred years old.

If you ever wondered what it would be like to walk down a street full of Wright houses, here is your chance. Within a block or two of Wright's Studio in Oak Park are fourteen of his buildings. The photographs we usually see of these works show them individually, but there are many surprises to experiencing them in their neighborhoods. For instance, to see the Mrs. Thomas Gale House shoehorned between two larger houses is as much of a shock as seeing the Robie House sitting on an urban corner lot rather than in a spacious prairie all by itself. From the vantage point of the sidewalk next to the three-story Fricke House, you will realize that not all of the Prairie houses hug the ground in the same way.

A personal visit to the Oak Park area is a delightful eye-opener for Frank Lloyd Wright fans. A trip along the lakeshore north of Chicago on Sheridan Road leads past five Frank Lloyd Wright houses. The Willits House in Highland Park is the last in the line (northernmost) and the most grand. It sits on several acres with tall oaks in the background—an ideal site for a Prairie house.

Thanks to the many preservation groups, the ten buildings open to the public are well maintained, and many of the private residences are accessible through guided walking tours held from time to time.

Thomas A. Heinz
Unity Temple, June, 1992

FRANK LLOYD WRIGHT HOUSE
WEST FACADE

The oldest of Wright's buildings still standing, this was the first of his many residences. It has been reconfigured in recent years to resemble its appearance in 1911, when Wright last resided there. Even though the house was built during the Victorian era, there is little fussy detail and the clarity of the design comes through. The simple geometric shapes are clearly expressed in this facade. The triangle is set on a base of two octagonal bays joined at the center. The brick walls are curved in the arc of a circle and extend at the tangent to meet the wall of the house.

GEORGE BLOSSOM HOUSE
SOUTH ELEVATION

This house shows off Wright's ability in classical design. The inset of the central panel is one of the subtle but refreshing details that sets off Wright's approach from the more textbook copies of classical facades by other architects. This same fresh approach is reflected in the planning and details of the interior. The rooms in the front and rear are lined up in a row and joined together at the center of the living room and stairway, shown here inset between the library on the right and the dining room on the left. The space of the dining room is extended from the cube into the curved bay.

WARREN MCARTHUR HOUSE
SOUTH ENTRANCE

The entry is on the south side of the McArthur House. The classical ogee profile of the limestone base seems out of place on this Dutch colonial house, but arched doorways are as intriguing today as they were when this house was built. The brick color nearly matches the stucco, making a monochromatic statement, as did many of Wright's early commissions.

WILLIAM H. WINSLOW HOUSE
WEST ELEVATION

*E*ven though it is over a hundred years old, this design still looks modern. The plain and simple walls, the clean colors of the iron-spot brick, and the contrasting limestone trim all contribute to its timelessness. The symmetry of the facade recalls the classical feeling without copying earlier designs. This short, wide doorway fools us into thinking the house is much larger than it really is. The small terracotta flower urns were the first of what became a Wright trademark detail between 1900 and 1915.

WILLIAM H. WINSLOW HOUSE
FRONT DOOR DETAIL

The limestone door detail is similar to those that were popular at the 1893 World's Fair—reinterpretations of Greek details into midwestern motifs using abstractions of corn, wheat, burr oak leaves, and sumac. The wooden door carvings based on oak leaves are executed in a style that was used by Louis Sullivan, Wright's former employer and mentor. The cotyledon, or seed pod, symbolized life and growth.

13

Chauncey L. Williams House
East Elevation Detail

The ornamental window to the left of the door is an example of Wright's interest in traditional design. The cut fretwork within the arch over the door is obscured by a thick buildup of paint, accumulated over nearly a hundred years since the house was built. Local lore has it that the boulders flanking the door were gathered from the nearby Des Plaines River personally by Wright, Williams, and two of his neighbors who were also Wright clients—Winslow and Waller.

NATHAN G. MOORE HOUSE
EAST FACADE

The bottom portion of this house was designed by Wright in 1895. A devastating Christmas-night fire in 1923 burned the top off the house, and Wright was engaged to redesign the upper house for Moore, his attorney during his early career. The Gothic bay window was not designed by Wright. Some of the terracotta ornamentations installed by Wright in 1923 are duplicates of Sullivan designs. No one is quite sure how they became part of the construction. The detail on the edge of the barge board is typical of Wright's work of the 1920s.

ISADORE HELLER HOUSE
EAST FACADE

From written color notes, we know that the Heller House was monochromatic, as were the Husser and Winslow houses. The Heller had a closely toned orange tile roof and russet plaster frieze. The alternating bands of brick on the second floor were done in advance of an article written by Sullivan on tapestry brick.

FRANK THOMAS HOUSE
WEST ELEVATION

Light gray stucco and olive green trim was the original color scheme. By Wright's definition of a Prairie house, this was the first: the main rooms are all on the upper floor; there is no basement; a ribbon window circles the girth. The low-pitched roof and overhanging eaves are also characteristics of the Prairie house. With these items defined, Prairie could become a style, but in analyzing Wright's houses of the era, few actually fit the definition.

ARTHUR HEURTLEY HOUSE
WEST ELEVATION

Heurtley was a banker. This house gives the unmistakable appearance of a fortress. The second owner of the house was Andrew Porter, Wright's brother-in-law. Much of the original furniture went with the Porters when they moved to Tani-deri at Taliesin in Wisconsin. The stucco panel in front of the living room matches the original color. Here also is a very creative use of tapestry brick. The brick prow in front of the arched doorway at one time had two terra-cotta flower urns like those at the Ward Willits House.

23

WARD W. WILLITS HOUSE
FULL FACADE

The Ward W. Willits House is the true masterpiece of all of Wright's Prairie houses. This is the way it was meant to be. It is a long, low building flung far into the landscape. Low-pitched roofs with wide overhangs offer a sheltering repose. The cross-axial plan and abundant windows provide views from all rooms and invite refreshing cross-breezes. Horizontality is dominant, and yet the house is highlighted by the central pavilion. Not strictly symmetrical, the balance is maintained by the flow of the line. The building is angular without being severe. All of the rooms are expressed on the exterior, but they are not exposed because the art-glass patterns maintain privacy. It is no surprise, then, that Mr. Willits lived in the house for over fifty years. How could one move out of such a perfect work of art?

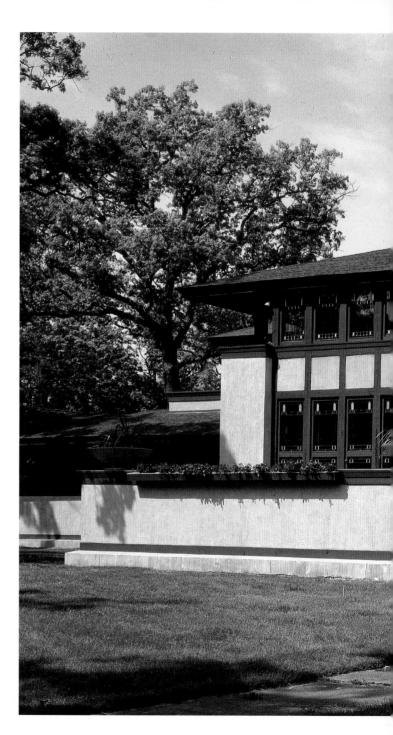

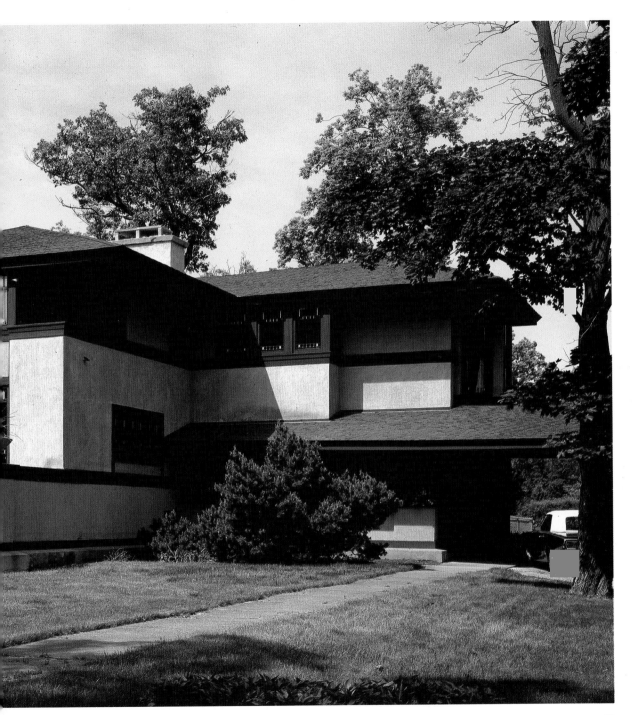

WARD W. WILLITS HOUSE
WEST PORCH DETAIL

Dutch doors here are surprisingly refreshing. The tops of these doors are nearly at ceiling level, making a good escape route for hot air. The distance between the top of the Dutch doors and the bottom of the upper windows makes it difficult to determine the actual distance between floors. This ambiguity then throws off the sense of scale, making it hard to evaluate the actual size of the building. A small area of peeling paint shows that the original color of the house was egg-shell brown.

E. Arthur Davenport House
West Elevation

The original design of the Davenport House was similar to the "House with Lots of Room in It" as published in the *Ladies' Home Journal*. The roof extended out over a bay, and a porch extended from the living room, similar to that of the Willits House. The entry canopy on the left has a very Japanese feeling to it. This is one of a few houses that Wright designed with his only partner, Webster Tomlinson.

William G. Fricke House
North Elevation

Although this is one of Wright's Prairie houses, the typical definition of that style seems inappropriate for this tall house. The wide stairs lead up to the front door that is behind the plain wall to the right. Vertical windows light the inside stairwell leading to the second floor. Inside the prow is the music, or reception, room. At one time, a stucco wall connected the garage on the left to the house. The spindles at the left conceal an outside porch.

WILLIAM G. FRICKE HOUSE
DINING ROOM

The details in this house are fascinating. The ceiling trim and the upper wall trim are larger, and there is a greater amount of trim in this house than in most other Wright houses. The arrangement of spindles in the panel on the right is unusual—square spindles set on the diagonal with thin strips of wood between them. The wall sconces are composed of a metal cube enclosing the bulb socket mounted on a wooden oak square that is framed in cast-bronze angle. This style of sconce was used in many of the Prairie era houses. Wright designed a dining room set for this home. The table, which is an octagonal leg extension table, is now at the Victoria and Albert Museum in London.

WILLIAM E. MARTIN HOUSE
WEST ELEVATION

Another example of a tall Prairie house, this one once had a lovely garden to the south, a site now occupied by a newer house. The third floor is a children's playroom with a very low headline trim. William Martin's brother, Darwin D. Martin of Buffalo, visited William in Oak Park in September 1902 and toured the Wright buildings. Darwin related to Elbert Hubbard that "Wright could make $8,000 look like $15,000 in a house."

WILLIAM E. MARTIN HOUSE
LIVING ROOM

The double ceiling trim is unique. One band rings the room and the other appears to pierce the wall and follow into the adjoining room. The built-in bench next to the fireplace and the one on the left precluded the introduction of other furniture and helped to keep the floor space from being cluttered. With more usable floor space, then, a small room appears to be much larger.

WILLIAM E. MARTIN HOUSE
ENTRY HALL

The art-glass ceiling light runs uninterrupted into the reception area and under the crossbar. Wright's skill at making walled space seem larger by extending the visual presentation into other rooms is reinforced with this technique. This is certainly one way to get what appears to be more house for the money.

EDWIN H. CHENEY HOUSE
WEST ELEVATION

Although the tall house to the north makes the Cheney house appear to be very short, it has a full basement under the main floor, and the porch parapet walls are set quite low. Mrs. Cheney left her family and Wright left his; they traveled to Europe together in 1909 so Wright could complete his major portfolio published by Ernst Wasmuth. The book made Wright famous, while the trip made him infamous. Soon after their return, Wright built Taliesin at Spring Green and the couple settled there.

PETER A. BEACHY HOUSE
WEST FACADE

This is a house of seven gables, although there is no evidence that any conscious effort was made to relate this to the building of literary renown. The scale of this house is very large, possibly indicating that the original owner was quite tall. This house was termed a remodeling because an earlier house is incorporated inside. The most unusual thing about this structure is the use of a variety of materials: brick, concrete, stucco, and wood trim. Because of its proportioning, many have thought that the home was designed by Walter Burley Griffin, employed by Wright, but the latest analysis points to Wright as the designer.

UNITY TEMPLE
WEST FACADE

The design concept of this church comes from a Japanese temple, where the people and the priests enter at the center and go to their separate sides. The columns hold part of the weight of the roof. Behind the roof parapet is a pyramidal skylight that is the weather shield over the art-glass panels seen from the temple interior. The original budget for Unity Temple was $40,000—a low figure even at that time. The concrete for the exterior was washed off, exposing some of the aggregate and giving it a rough texture.

45

UNITY TEMPLE INTERIOR

This assembly hall makes the most of limited space. Unlike most other religious rooms, this one utilizes three levels in order to achieve a higher person-to-cubic-foot ratio. It also places more of the worshipers close to the minister to give them a greater feeling of intimacy during the proceedings. Wright likely learned the understanding of performance spaces from his former employer, Dankmar Adler of Adler and Sullivan, while designing the Auditorium, Schiller Theater, Anshe Marav Synagogue, and other assembly buildings.

F. F. Tomek House
South Facade

Clearly this is the forerunner for the Robie House. This is not to say that Wright designed the Tomek House with a later version in mind, but the two buildings are strikingly similar, especially in the plan of their main floors, their pavilion of bedrooms at the top of the houses, their south facades having ribbon windows, and their low-pitched roofs. The central entry on the front facade of the Tomek House is a rarity in the Prairie era— bringing people into the center of the second, or main, floor. The living room is to the right, and the dining room is to the left with the kitchen behind.

AVERY COONLEY HOUSE
MOSAIC FRIEZE DETAIL

This frieze is located on the facade at the first floor grade and on the second floor. The ceramic tiles make an abstract pattern of a tulip. Incised lines in the concrete hold the tiles in place. It is a very unique installation that resulted in durable beauty.

Isabel Roberts House
West Elevation

Wright's secretary and her mother commissioned Wright to design this small house in 1906. In the 1950s Wright did a marvelous job of updating his own design by adding the brick and a wood ceiling as part of a remodeling. A close look reveals a tree growing through the back of the roof of the porch on the left.

ISABEL ROBERTS HOUSE
LIVING ROOM

Introducing Usonian details into a Prairie-era house was a success. The ceiling is reminiscent of that of the David Wright House in Phoenix. The head height of the balcony is at a minimum. A built-in desk lies directly behind the balcony wall. The dimensions indicate that this is technically a one-and-a-half-story space, but it is needed in such a small house as spatial relief.

FREDERICK C. ROBIE HOUSE
SOUTH FACADE

As with many brick houses of Wright's Prairie era, this house has been changed from Wright's original design through remodeling. Several walls have since been lowered and the original mortar colors and brick-laying techniques have been obliterated by insensitive maintenance and uninformed "restoration." The low wall on the right was originally much higher and formed a motor court in front of the garages. Now, as with Unity Temple and many houses, the landscaping obscures the buildings.

Mrs. Thomas Gale House
North Elevation

This house is located behind the Peter Beachy House that faces Forest Avenue. Although it was designed during the height of Wright's renown, it does not have the characteristic Prairie elements. There are no low-pitched roofs with overhanging eaves on all sides. There are groups of windows, but there are no long strips of them. While not a Prairie style house, it's a remarkably forward-looking design along the same lines as Wright's famous Fallingwater.

E. D. Brigham House
East Elevation

Based on the important design found in the fireproof house for $5,000 (also known as the Four-Square Plan) published in the *Ladies' Home Journal* and nearly duplicated in the Steven Hunt House of LaGrange, this example is constructed of concrete. It is a large house covering over a hundred feet from eaves to eaves. The central pavilion is divided, with the living room occupying the front half, the dining room the left rear, and the kitchen the remaining quarter. The porch on the south and the porte cochere on the north break its boxy appearance.

Lloyd Lewis House
South Facade

By far the majority of Wright's designs in Chicagoland were constructed between 1889 and 1912. There were only six out of more than a hundred built in Chicago and its suburbs after 1920. The house is raised above grade to protect it from potential flooding of the adjacent Des Plaines River. Mr. Lewis was a highly regarded reporter for the *Chicago Daily News*. The house is easier to reach by canoe down the river than by car through twisty, unmarked roads and drives, making the property wonderfully private.

❦ These properties are open for public tours.